Sea Beavers & Rattle Slugs
Stories and pictures by Rae Grout
and dedicated to her loving son Steven

This is a humorous journey designed to tickle the heart and bring a smile to the reader's face. The short stories in this book are based on real life experiences of the animal kingdom and new environments experienced in life's little adventures shared with my son.

I would like to thank all the members of my wonderful family for making this whimsical journey possible.

I would also like to thank Woodland Park Zoo for their wonderful environment and allowing me to express the fun days my son and I had in their magnificent park.

Thanks for the memories :-)

D1263007

Contents

Sea Beavers

Steven was 4 years old when we moved from the mountains and countryside of Montana to the bustling city of Seattle. The sites and sounds of a city at sea level are much different than the sites and sounds of the mountains and streams he had been used to. Steven had seen an abundance of wildlife while living in Montana such as deer, fox, pheasant and an occasional beaver as we floated the slow and lazy Madison River.

One evening after dinner Steven and I had been walking on a pier off the shores of Lake Washington. In the distance we heard a splashing sound in the water. This sound was a fun and playful one that made us curious about who or what could be making such amusing play. As we quietly approached the lighthearted splashes we stooped down low not wanting to scare whomever away. A silhouette of a small critter could be seen in the water under the dim lights of the pier.

We silently watched for several minutes when Steven put his little arm around me and whispered in my ear. "Momma, that's a sea beaver". I was giggling under my breath too hard to tell him our little water friend was actually an otter.

Rattle Slugs

Steven was outside on a warm sunny day blowing bubbles in his bear slippers. This was one of his favorite pastimes. In fact I carried bubbles with us wherever we went. This really paid off when we had been stuck in traffic. On one occasion we had been stuck on one of the floating bridges for hours but Steven shared his bubbles with our neighboring commuter friends and we all had a lovely time until traffic was able to move again.

On this sunny day the bubbles seemed to glide dangerously close to the ground almost clipping the poky grass, then catching a light breeze and pulling up out of harm's way into a gentle puff of wind, then off up into the sky.

Steven studied one bubble as it dangerously began to drift over the grass then looked in horror as he saw a scary creature lurking under the rose bushes. Dropping his bubble wand, Steven ran into the house and grabbed me as if to bring his mother into the realization of a new discovery. "Momma, this place has Rattle Slugs."

I held back my chuckles and put on a serious face as I went to inspect the grounds with my son. Sure enough there he was with spots and stripes like a little rattlesnake in a slug suit. I knelt down and petted the slug's cool skin and softly told Steven this is a friendly little guy and not part of the snake family at all.

Cotton Candy Skies

Every year I would purchase three annual passes for Steven and me. One was a pass to the Museum of Flight, one to the Pacific Science Center and one was a Surf and Turf pass. The Surf and Turf pass allowed access to both Woodland Park Zoo and the Seattle Aquarium.

Steven and I would spend an entire Saturday either enjoying Seattle's waterfront or walking the wonderful paths of Woodland Park Zoo. We loved the animal sounds and taking in the educational exhibits.

On one magical morning we were winding our way down one of the many paths and a light puff of cotton candy blew over our heads. As we walked further down the path more and more cotton candy was blowing in the light breeze. Steven and I were able to chase and snatch the whimsical treat out of the air like little kids jumping after bubbles. Cotton candy was in the trees and people's hair as they walked by. Laughter and joy was in the air as well and all because a vendor mistakenly put his machine out doors to enjoy the day. The vendor did not realize a light breeze could have such a sense of humor and whisk his product into the air filling the sky with cotton candy.

Chalker Stalker

I had been studying art through one of the local art schools. They had a program in the spring and fall seasons that allowed students to enter the zoo early in the morning before the gates opened to the public. This enabled the artist to study the animals and their movements in the peaceful early mornings. The wonderful art instructor we had would teach us to look for the animal's rhythm of life and try and capture this in our sketches. Through the eyes of an artist saw much more than animals in enclosures. I saw the interaction between man and wild beast. Nowhere else could children see such magnificent animals up close and learn about their habitats.

I also saw behind the scenes and how these animals are cared for and loved by their keepers. When we entered the zoo we could only use environmentally safe materials to draw and illustrate with. This narrowed our selection down to using natural charcoals or pastels. Because the pastels looked like chalk the children who visited the zoo regularly and saw me with my big drawing board and pastels called me a Chalker.

One cold autumn day I had been sitting outside an exhibit for hours sketching animals' movements and absorbed in their interactions. My instructor came by and quietly whispered in my ear, "You are being stalked". I looked at the exhibit and could not see who could be stalking me. She said, "Turn around." Behind me there was a chain link fence and lying quietly in the bushes was a beautiful snow leopard. My instructor said he had been watching me all day. He had a sweet face and almost seemed to smile when I finally looked at him. Later on when I recounted the story to my son, he said, "Cool Mom, a Chalker Stalker". From that day on snow leopards have been known as Chalker Stalkers between Steven and me.

Pygmy Marmosets

One of Steven's favorite exhibits at the zoo was the pygmy marmosets and the tamarins. Pygmy marmosets, the world's tiniest monkeys, were little hams when it came to drawing their portraits. The one on the following page picked out a branch to sit on as I stood behind the glass window to draw him. He occasionally came up to the glass as if to ask about my progress. I would turn my big drawing board around and he studied it for some time then returned to his branch to pose again.

The tamarin, a close relative of the pygmy marmoset and seen below would watch closely as the pygmy marmoset sat on his branch. The tamarin would periodically scold the pygmy marmoset for fraternizing with humans.

Steven loved these little primates and thought they looked like little pirates because of the identification tags that appeared to be small hooped earrings in one ear.

Pallas's Cat

One morning when I entered the zoo for my drawing class I could hear a soft crying sound in the distance. I followed a long winding path towards the sound. It was a cold autumn day and only a few artists had arrived at the zoo. The gates had not opened to the public yet so with the place virtually empty the sound was easy to track.

As I rounded the corner of the cat exhibits the sound became louder and more profound. At the backside of the exhibit was a large area with rocks and trees. This was the home of the Pallas's cat. An animal that was a little larger than a house cat. She was in the exhibit rubbing her head against the rocks and crying in sad little whimpers along with soft little howls. The sounds she had been making broke my heart so I started to talk softly to her. She looked my way seeming to respond to my caring voice.

Her keeper came out to greet me. She said the cat's name was Ling Ling and her mate had just passed away. The Pallas's cat was mourning the loss of her friend. When the keeper walked off Ling Ling came over and lay on a large rock in front of me. I pulled out my drawing board and began to sketch and talk to her as if she were an old friend.

The gates finally opened to the public. I could tell Ling Ling did not like people who were noisy and obnoxious. When people became too loud she would scamper back to her cave to hide until they were gone. Luckily for me it was a cold day and not too many people were at the zoo. Once the noisy people had left she would come back to her rock and let me tell her how beautiful she was and how sorry I was about the loss of her friend. At the end of the day, right before the gates closed, I blew her a kiss and wished her a much happier future. There comes a time in everyone's life when a comforting voice and an open heart can help put all creatures large and small back on the road to happiness.

The Wave

A wave is not just a hand motion
but an extension of one's soul.
It reaches out to another, embraces and takes hold.

For a brief moment in time it says,
I acknowledge you and I care.
An emotional investment if you dare.

I had a neighbor, we communicated in waves,
as neighbors meet when their children play.

One day he was suddenly gone.
From our lives he was ripped away.
I thought of all the lost opportunities of future waves.

Please do not take this hand motion for granted.
Never hesitate to wave.

For the emotional investment is far less costly
Than the opportunity lost in one missed wave.

Love and dedication to Walt Kilgore

Momma's Boots

Momma's boots have been to weddings,
rodeos and stock car races.

Momma's glad those boots can't talk.
They must have been in some secret
places.

I use her boots for hiding things,
cars, trucks and my little dozer.

Momma knows when her keys are missing,
just grab a boot and turn it over.

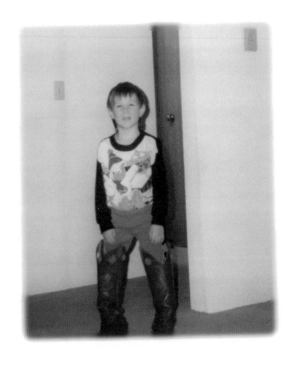

Momma's Shoulders

Riding on Momma's shoulders
weaving through the crowds.
"Giddy up," Steven giggles out loud.

Up where light breezes blow through Steve's hair.
He can see the entire world from up there.

Momma's shoulders hold her son high
and out of harm's way.
Her shoulders will always be there
for him.
Long after this day.

Adiós Flamingos

Adiós Flamingos ~
Night Night my sweet son
May you always be comfortable.
May life always be fun.

I hope you soar like an eagle.
Your limit's the sky.

Just never drive faster,
than your guardian angel
can fly.

250814